The Little Book of FRIENDSHIP

By Zack Bush and Laurie Friedman
Illustrated by Sarah Van Evera

DEDICATED TO YOU—
OUR WONDERFUL READER

THIS BOOK BELONGS TO OUR FRIEND :

_____

FRIENDSHIPS are like flowers.
They start out as tiny seeds.

But if you take care of
them, they grow and bloom until
you have a beautiful garden.

Making a FRIEND is
as easy as being one.

Not sure how?
No worries!
There are so
many ways
to show
someone you
want to be
their FRIEND.

TURN THE PAGE TO
FIND OUT MORE! ⟹

A great place to start is
by saying, "Hi, my name is _____."

And before you know it . . .
you will have a FRIEND.

You can use your words to make FRIENDS.
There are so many good ones to choose from.

WHICH WORDS WOULD YOU CHOOSE?

WANT TO PLAY?

WAY TO GO! GREAT

I'M GLAD WE

LET'S SHARE!

THIS WAS FUN!

LET'S DO IT AGAIN!

JOB! THANKS FOR HELPING!

ARE FRIENDS!

YOU'RE AMAZING!

Doing nice things for others is a great way to be a FRIEND. You can . . .

Invite your FRIEND to your house.

Play what your FRIEND wants to play.

Share your toys.

Laugh when your FRIEND tells a joke.

What does it mean
to be a good FRIEND?

Pitching in if someone needs help . . .

And lending a hand if they get hurt.

Cheering a person up if they're down . . .

And encouraging them
to keep going when
they want to give up.

Complimenting someone
when they do a good job . . .

And never being afraid to say, "I'm sorry."

Being a good FRIEND means
accepting and appreciating that
FRIENDS may be different than you.

You can learn new things from your FRIENDS.

You can have lots of fun with your FRIENDS.

WHAT WOULD YOU LIKE TO DO WITH YOUR FRIENDS?

Play catch

Draw pictures

Ride bikes

Bake cookies

Climb a tree

Blow bubbles

What are some things that a FRIEND can do?

Sit quietly beside you when
you don't feel like talking . . .

And include you,
even if they're
playing with
someone else.

Being a FRIEND means never ever making
fun of anyone. Even if they're scared.

SCARY THINGS

And always showing that you care.

And remember: The key to
having a **FRIEND** is being a **FRIEND**.

CONGRATULATIONS!

You've earned your

FRIENDSHIP BADGE.

Now you know so many

ways to be a good friend.

Go to the website
www.BooksByZackAndLaurie.com
to print out your patience badge.
And keep reading all of the books in
#thelittlebookof
series to learn new things
and earn more badges.

Other books in the series:

The Little Book of Camping
The Little Book of Patience
The Little Book of Kindness
The Little Book of Presidential Elections

Made in the USA
Monee, IL
19 September 2022